W9-CBT-228

Curious George®
Dinosaur Tracks

**Adaptation by Julie Tibbott
Based on the TV series teleplay written
by Bruce Akiyama**

Houghton Mifflin Harcourt Publishing Company
Boston New York

Copyright © 2011 Universal Studios. Curious George and related characters, created by Margret and H. A. Rey, are copyrighted and trademarked by Houghton Mifflin Harcourt Publishing Company and used under license. *Curious George* television series merchandise licensed by Universal Studios Licensing LLLP. All rights reserved. The PBS KIDS logo is a registered trademark of PBS and is used with permission. Green Light Readers and its logo are trademarks of Houghton Mifflin Harcourt Publishing Company.

For information about permission to reproduce selections from this book, write to Permissions, Houghton Mifflin Harcourt Publishing Company, 215 Park Avenue South, New York, New York 10003.

Library of Congress Cataloging-in-Publication Data is on file.

ISBN: 978-0-547-44960-9 paper-over-board
ISBN: 978-0-547-43888-7 paperback

Design by Afsoon Razavi

www.hmhco.com

Printed in China
SCP 10 9 8 7 6 5 4
4500585193

Ages: 5-7
Grade: 2
Guided Reading Level: J
Reading Recovery Level: 17

George was curious about animal
tracks.
He took photos of raccoon, frog,
and squirrel tracks.

"Wow!" said Bill.
"You have almost
every local animal except the fawn.
Come on! I'll show you where to find it."

A fawn is a baby deer.
It would make the perfect photo.

Bill took George to the place he saw
the fawn.
"Good luck," he said. "After I finish fixing
the path, I'm going swimming in the lake."

George looked for
fawn tracks.
The first track he found was from
a slithery garter snake.

Then he found duck
and frog tracks.
They both have webbed feet. That must
be why they are good swimmers.

George saw that fish do not
leave any tracks!

Then George found the biggest
tracks he had seen yet!
Could the tracks be from a giant
snake with duck feet?
George followed the tracks.

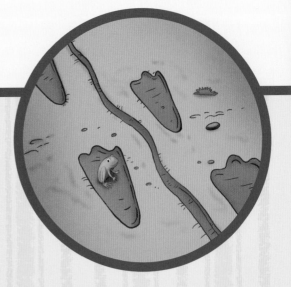

They ended at the
lake. George had an idea.
He had seen these tracks in a book.
They were dinosaur tracks!

He made a trail of food back to his house.
Maybe the dinosaur would come out to eat.
Then George could take a photo.

But wait! George went home to
look at the book.
Some dinosaurs eat meat. Uh-oh.
Maybe they would eat him!

George went
back to the water.
He saw the tracks were now
coming out of the lake!

The tracks were headed toward
Bill's house.
George had to warn Bill!

"I guess those do look like dinosaur
tracks," Bill said.
"But I made the tracks."

"I went swimming with my flippers.
I had my rake too."
George was happy that Bill left the tracks.
A hungry dinosaur would be scary!

George still wanted a special photo.
The trail of food that led to the lake
was still there.

Suddenly, the fawn showed up
to eat the food . . . with the
mama deer!

It was the perfect picture to complete George's collection—even if it was not a dinosaur!

Animal Tracks

Look at the animals and their matching tracks.

What do you think George's tracks look like?

Making Tracks!

Did you know that you can make plaster casts of animal tracks? Next time you and an adult find an animal track while on a hike, in a park, or exploring your own backyard, try it—it's fun and easy!

What you will need:

Plaster of Paris (found at craft stores), a bottle of water, plastic spoons, paper towels, a plastic container or paper cups to mix the plaster, a small trowel or something to dig with, paint, a backpack to carry everything in, and a grownup to help.

Making Tracks!

What to do:

1. Find a good, clean animal track in mud that has dried enough to keep its shape when you press on it lightly.

2. Lay out all your supplies. Pour about 3/4 cup of plaster into the plastic container. Quickly stir in water until the plaster is thin enough to pour, yet not too runny. Tap on the edge of the container to get out most of the air bubbles. Do this quickly, because the plaster begins to set within a few seconds.

3. Carefully pour the plaster mixture into the track. Let the plaster set for at least a half hour.

4. When the plaster is firm, carefully dig under the cast and lift it up. Take it home and let it dry overnight.

5. When the plaster cast is completely dry, clean it off with a brush. You may want to paint the cast.

Now you have an animal track that will last forever!